My Best Book of

The Moon

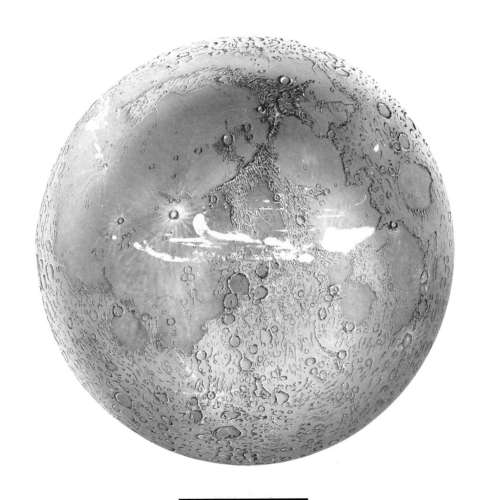

Ian Graham

KINGFISHER

Author: Ian Graham
Senior editor: Sarah Milan
Series editor: Sue Nicholson
Designer: Malcolm Parchment
Production controller: Caroline Jackson
Illustrators: Ray Grinaway,
   Roger Stewart
Photographs: John Frassanito and
   Associates/NASA (page 30)

KINGFISHER
Kingfisher Publications Plc,
New Penderel House,
283–288 High Holborn,
London WC1V 7HZ
www.kingfisherpub.com

First published by Kingfisher
Publications Plc 1999
First published in paperback 2001

(hb) 10 9 8 7 6 5 4 3 2
2TR / 1298 / WKT / MAR(MAR) / 128MA
(pb) 10 9 8 7 6 5 4 3 2 1
1TR / 1000 / WKT / MAR(MAR) / 128KMA

Copyright © Kingfisher
Publications Plc 1999

A CIP catalogue record for this book
is available from the British Library.

ISBN 0 7534 0305 6 (hb)
       0 7534 0416 8 (pb)

Printed in Hong Kong / China

Contents

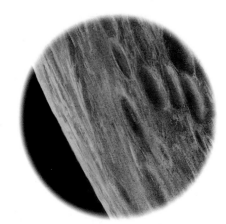
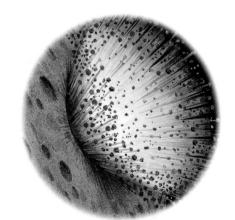

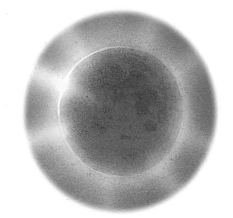

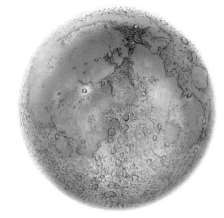

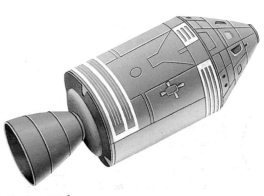

The magical Moon

In ancient times, many people worshipped the Moon as a god or goddess. The ancient Romans called their moon goddess Luna. The ancient Egyptians worshipped the moon god Khonsu. Other people did not believe the Moon was sacred but still thought it had magical powers. Some believed that a full, round Moon could make wolves howl and send people mad, or "moonstruck". Today, most people do not believe the Moon has special powers, but they are still fascinated by its mysterious beauty.

Moon legends

In many countries, legends and folk stories told of a man in the Moon, who had been put there for stealing.

Other people saw animal shapes, such as a cat, frog or hare, in the markings on the Moon's face.

Moon-watching

Astronomers study the Moon through powerful telescopes. Some telescopes are built inside domes on the tops of high mountains. The domes protect the telescopes from the wind, rain and snow. Far above car fumes, factory smoke and bright city lights, the air is cleaner and clearer. This gives astronomers a better view of the night sky. You do not need a powerful telescope to study the Moon, however. You can learn a lot by simply watching it with the naked eye.

Daytime Moon

The Moon rises and sets like the Sun. You can sometimes see it in the sky during the day. However, it is harder to spot at daytime because the Sun's light makes the sky very bright and the Moon seems to fade from view.

Moon-watching with
the naked eye ...

... with binoculars ...

... and with a
small telescope

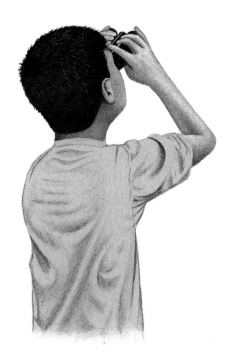

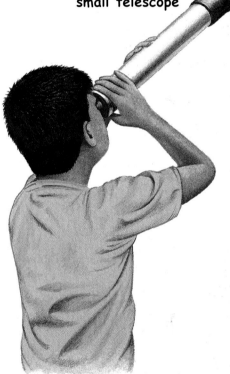

Naked eye

At night, you can see the Moon easily with the naked eye. You can watch it change shape from night to night, and see patches of light and dark on its surface.

Binoculars

A pair of binoculars makes the Moon seem much bigger and closer than it really is. With binoculars, you can see mountains on the Moon, and hollows, called craters.

Telescope

A small telescope helps you discover even more. You can see hundreds of smaller craters, the walls of larger craters, and shadows cast by the Moon's mountains.

Mountain-top observatory

The Moon in space

The Moon is our closest neighbour in space, but it is still far, far away. It is the biggest thing we can see in the sky simply because it is much closer to us than anything else. The Moon seems to glow, but it doesn't give out any light of its own. We only see it because it reflects, or casts back, light from the Sun shining on its surface.

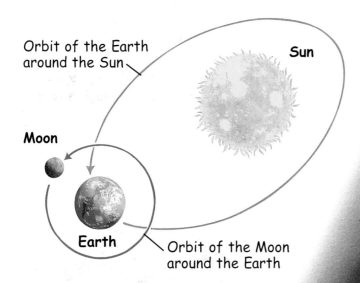

Orbit of the Earth around the Sun

Sun

Moon

Earth

Orbit of the Moon around the Earth

The Moon in motion

The Moon travels around the Earth and the Earth travels around the Sun in endless looping paths, called orbits.

Sun, Earth and Moon
spinning through space

What we see

As the Moon orbits the
Earth, part or all of its
face is lit up by the Sun.
From Earth, it seems as
though the Moon changes
shape from night to night,
but it is in fact always round.

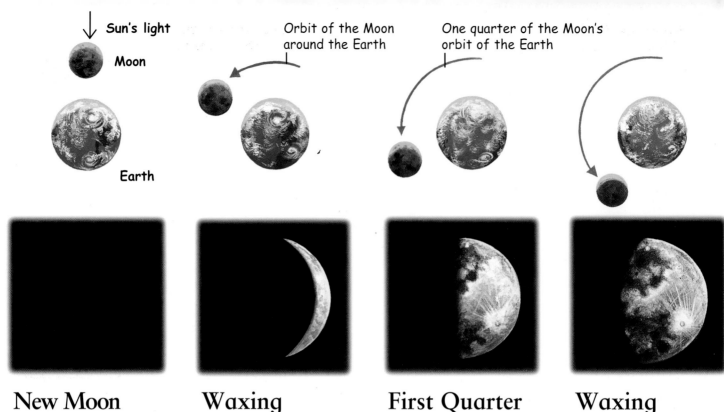

New Moon
The sunlit part of the Moon is turned away from the Earth and the Moon looks dark.

Waxing Crescent
A day or so later, one thin edge of the Moon is lit up and we see a crescent.

First Quarter
After a week, the Moon has travelled one quarter of its orbit of Earth and we see a Half Moon.

Waxing Gibbous
A few days later, we see more of the Moon's face, or a Gibbous Moon.

Phases of the Moon

The changes in the shape of the Moon are called the phases of the Moon. The Moon changes from a New Moon to a Full Moon and back again once every 29 and a half days, or lunar month. When the Moon looks as though it is growing bigger, we say it is waxing. When it seems to be shrinking, we say it is waning.

Moon festivals
In some countries in Asia, people celebrate the beauty of the Moon during the eighth lunar month, when it seems to be brighter than at any other time of the year. Children wear moon masks and carry glowing lanterns.

Half of the Moon's orbit of the Earth

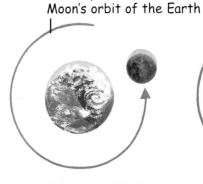

Three quarters of the Moon's orbit of the Earth

Full Moon
At Full Moon, the Moon is halfway round its orbit and the whole of the Moon's face is lit.

Waning Gibbous
After Full Moon, the Moon begins to wane and we see less of its face.

Last Quarter
A week after Full Moon, we see a Half Moon again and the Moon enters its Last Quarter.

Waning Crescent
As it completes its orbit, we see one thin edge of the Moon again.

The mid-autumn Moon festival in Vietnam, Asia

Eclipses

The Earth and the Moon cast long, dark shadows into space. Sometimes, as the Earth orbits the Sun, it passes between the Sun and the Moon. When this happens it casts a dark shadow across the Moon's surface. This is known as an eclipse of the Moon, or a lunar eclipse. The Moon doesn't disappear but turns a coppery colour. When the Moon passes between the Earth and the Sun, it blocks out the Sun's light for a few minutes. This is called an eclipse of the Sun, or a solar eclipse.

Total solar eclipse

During a total solar eclipse, the Moon's shadow covers the whole of the Sun's face. The corona – the Sun's outer atmosphere – then lights up. Normally, we cannot see the corona because the Sun's light is so bright. Scientists travel from all over the world to observe a solar eclipse.

Watching an eclipse

You must never look directly at the Sun. Its fierce light can severely damage your eyes. A good way of seeing a solar eclipse is to watch its reflection in a bowl of water.

Turn to page 31 for a list of solar and lunar eclipses for your diary

Type of eclipse

During a solar eclipse, we see a total eclipse of the Sun from the area of the Earth completely in the Moon's shadow. We see a partial eclipse of the Sun from the area of the Earth partly in the Moon's shadow.

Total eclipse seen from this part of the Earth

13

The Moon and tides

The oceans wash up onto the Earth's shores and fall back again twice every day. This movement of water, called the tide, is caused by the Moon's gravity, pulling the ocean and the Earth towards it. The Moon's "pull" forms a bulge of water on the side of Earth nearest the Moon and another on the opposite side of the Earth. These bulges of water move around the Earth, following the Moon, and produce the tides.

First high tide
When the Moon is above this town, it pulls the sea up towards the land, producing the day's first high tide.

Spring and neap tides
At Full or New Moon, the Moon and Sun line up with the Earth. The extra pull of gravity from the Sun makes higher (spring) tides. In the Moon's first and third quarters, the Sun's pull lessens the Moon's pull and makes lower (neap) tides.

First low tide

As the Earth turns, the Moon's pull becomes weak. The sea level falls and this gives the day's first low tide.

Second high tide

With the Moon on the opposite side of the Earth, a second bulge of water produces a second high tide.

Second low tide

The tide ebbs (goes out) as the Earth continues to turn and this brings about the day's second low tide.

Exploring the Moon

With the start of the Space Age in 1957, people began to learn more about the Moon. In 1959, a small space probe called Luna 2 became the first spacecraft to reach the Moon. Over the next ten years, dozens of different spacecraft circled the Moon, took photographs of it, and landed on its rocky surface. These unmanned space probes helped scientists find out whether it would be safe to send people to the Moon.

Surveyor 1 was the first spacecraft to land safely on the Moon

Safe landing

Seven Surveyor spacecraft were sent to the Moon. They showed that the Moon's surface was solid and safe to walk on.

Luna 2 was the first spacecraft to reach the Moon

The Eagle has landed

The famous words "the Eagle has landed" were spoken by Neil Armstrong on 20th July 1969, when his Apollo spacecraft, nicknamed "the Eagle", landed on the Moon. A few hours later, he became the first person to walk on the Moon. Between 1969 and 1972, the Apollo space project landed twelve astronauts on the Moon in seven separate Moon missions.

Gemini spacecraft
Many of the manoeuvres needed for a Moon landing had never been done before. Astronauts practised in the tiny two-person spacecraft, Gemini.

Apollo 14 Moon mission

Moonwalking

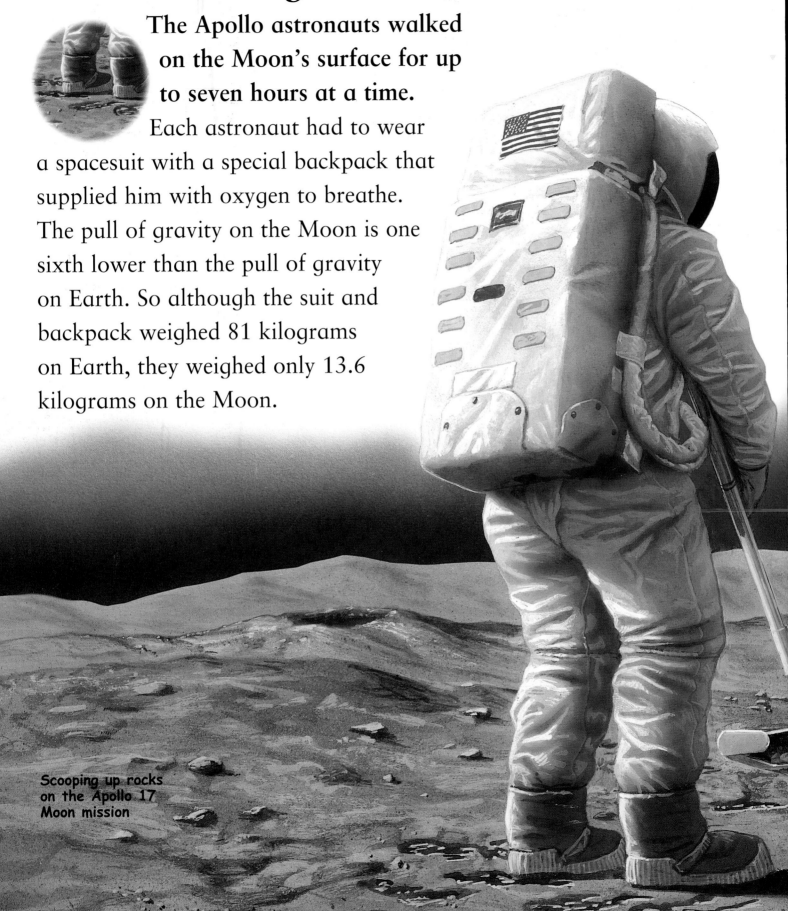

The Apollo astronauts walked on the Moon's surface for up to seven hours at a time. Each astronaut had to wear a spacesuit with a special backpack that supplied him with oxygen to breathe. The pull of gravity on the Moon is one sixth lower than the pull of gravity on Earth. So although the suit and backpack weighed 81 kilograms on Earth, they weighed only 13.6 kilograms on the Moon.

Scooping up rocks
on the Apollo 17
Moon mission

Giant steps
Astronauts had to practice how to walk in the Moon's weak gravity.

They had to think what to do a couple of step ahead so that they could stop or turn without falling over.

Each stride threw up clouds of fine dust which settled over the astronauts' legs and boots.

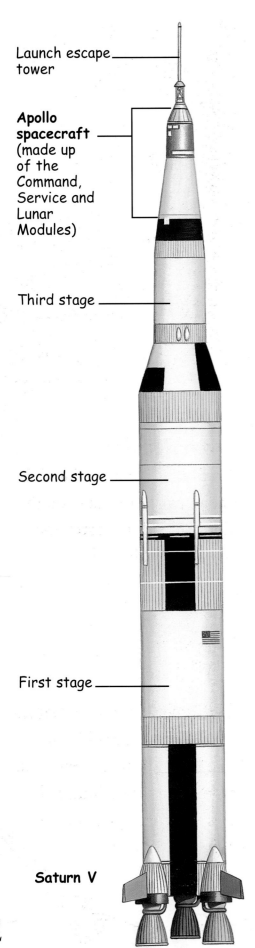

Launch escape tower

Apollo spacecraft (made up of the Command, Service and Lunar Modules)

Third stage

Second stage

First stage

Saturn V

Moon gear

The Apollo spacecraft were launched into space by the world's biggest rocket, the **Saturn V.** Saturn V stood 110 metres high and weighed nearly 3,000 tonnes. Most of this weight was fuel needed to blast the 50-tonne Apollo spacecraft to the Moon.

Saturn V rocket

Saturn V was made up of three rockets, called stages. When each stage used up its fuel, it fell away and the next stage took over.

Command Module

Service Module

Service Module engine

Command and Service Modules

Each three-man Apollo crew lived and worked inside the tiny cone-shaped Command Module. The Service Module supplied electricity, oxygen and water.

Instrument used to measure moonquakes

Solar panels to produce electricity from sunlight

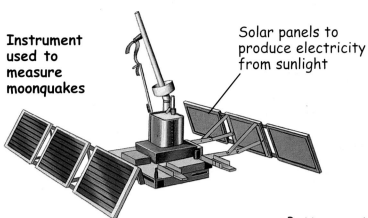

Lunar Module

Bottom part used as a platform to launch top part when leaving the Moon

Foot pads

Ladder

UNITED STATES

Moon experiments

Astronauts measured the Moon's temperature, detected moon-quakes, and used a laser mirror to measure the exact distance between the Earth and the Moon.

Aerial dish to carry astronaut's voice to Earth

Control panel

TV camera

Lunar Module

The Lunar Excursion Module landed two astronauts on the Moon. The third astronaut stayed in orbit in the Command Module.

Bags to hold rock samples

Moon Buggy

On the last three missions, astronauts used a Lunar Roving Vehicle, or Buggy, so they could travel further from the Lunar Module.

Wheels driven by electric motors and powered by batteries

Collecting Moon rocks

The astronauts could not bend down in their spacesuits, so they used long-handled tools with scoops or claws at the end to pick up rocks.

Claw opens and closes

The face of the Moon

The same side of the Moon always faces the Earth, so the pattern of light and dark patches we can see on its surface never changes. The darkest patches are flat, low plains formed by vast flows of molten, or melted, rock that cooled and hardened millions of years ago. These plains are called *maria*, meaning seas, but they do not contain water. The lighter areas are craters, mountains and valleys called rilles, all covered in a dusty moon rock called regolith.

Craters

Most of the Moon's surface is covered with thousands of craters, caused by rocks crashing into it from space.

Mountains

Mountains cover one sixth of the Moon's surface. These "highlands" are the oldest parts of the Moon.

Rilles

Rilles are long, narrow valleys, formed by cracks in the Moon's crust or carved out by rivers of lava.

Moon rocks

Breccia

Basalt

Holes made by gas escaping when rock was molten

Anorthosite

Moon history

Moon rocks and soil samples collected by astronauts have provided scientists with important clues about the Moon's history. Tests showed that the Moon's rocks are similar to rocks found all over the Earth. Because of this, scientists now think that the Moon may once have been part of the Earth.

Moon soil – containing tiny bits of rock and glass

Birth of the Moon

1 Some scientists believe the Moon was formed about four billion years ago, when the Earth was hit by a piece of rock as big as the planet Mars.

2 The collision blasted a huge amount of rock from Earth out into space. The shattered pieces of rock went into orbit around the Earth.

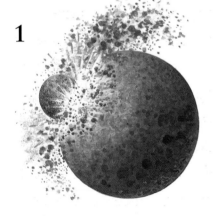

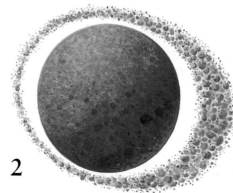

3 Over millions of years, the rocks clumped together to form the Moon. Molten lava gushed up onto the surface from deep inside, making the *maria*, or seas.

How a crater is formed

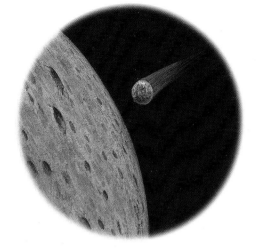

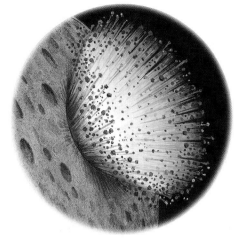

1 Most of the Moon's craters were made by asteroids, or space rocks, crashing into the seas or the middle of older craters.

2 Fierce heat made by the collision destroyed the original asteroid and shattered and melted the surrounding Moon rock.

3 Rock and dust flung up into space settled around a bowl-shaped crater. Some Moon craters are tiny. Others are 250 km wide.

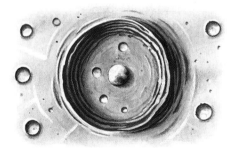

Terraced crater

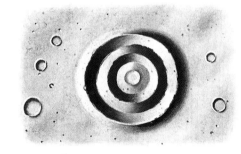

Concentric crater

Moon craters

Most Moon craters are simple bowl-shaped hollows with low rims. Others have steep, terraced sides with hills or mountains in the middle. Concentric craters look like rings inside rings. They may once have been volcanoes. Ray craters are surrounded by grey streaks, or rays, made by lighter coloured rocks. Older ghost craters have almost been filled in by molten rock.

Ray crater

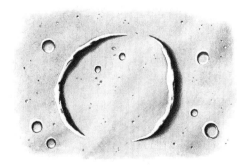

Ghost crater

Moon maps

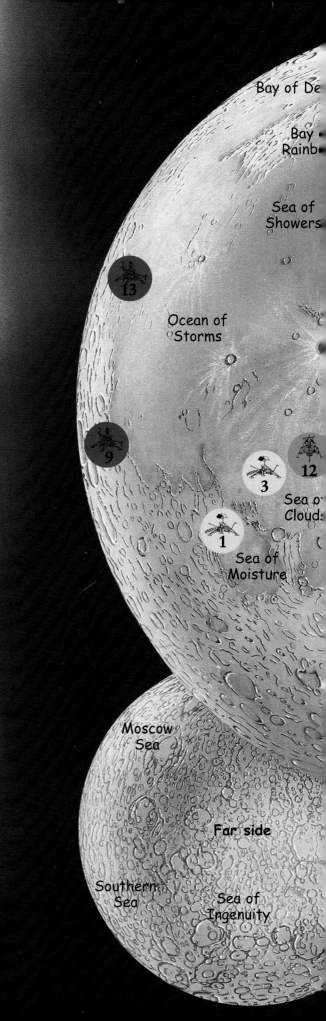

Early maps drawn by astronomers 400 years ago did not show all the Moon's craters and seas. This was because their telescopes were not very powerful. More detailed maps were made as telescopes became stronger. The most accurate Moon maps were made using photographs taken by space probes in the 1960s.

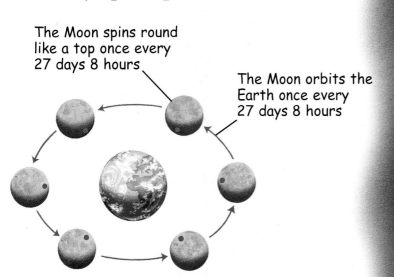

The Moon spins round like a top once every 27 days 8 hours

The Moon orbits the Earth once every 27 days 8 hours

Why we see one side

The Moon takes the same length of time to spin once as it does to travel all the way round the Earth. This means that the same side of the Moon always faces the Earth.

Bay of De

Bay Rainb

Sea of Showers

13

Ocean of Storms

9

12

3

Sea o Cloud

1

Sea of Moisture

Moscow Sea

Far side

Southern Sea

Sea of Ingenuity

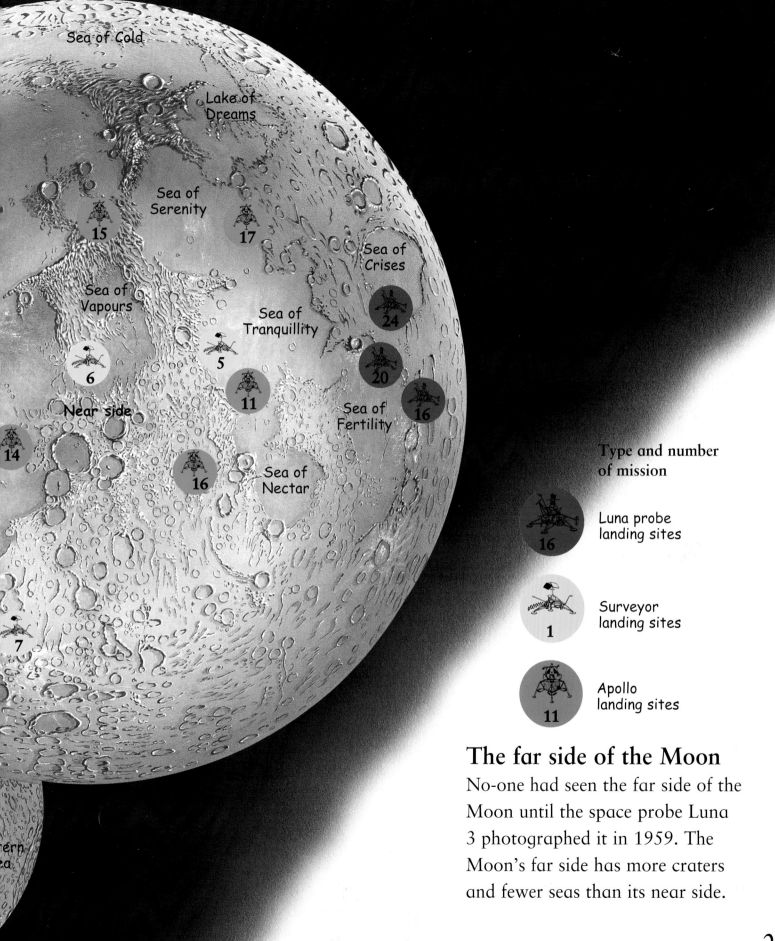

Sea of Cold

Lake of Dreams

Sea of Serenity

15

17

Sea of Crises

Sea of Vapours

Sea of Tranquillity

24

6

5

20

Near side

11

Sea of Fertility

16

14

16

Sea of Nectar

7

...ern ...a

Type and number of mission

Luna probe landing sites
16

Surveyor landing sites
1

Apollo landing sites
11

The far side of the Moon

No-one had seen the far side of the Moon until the space probe Luna 3 photographed it in 1959. The Moon's far side has more craters and fewer seas than its near side.

Moon bases

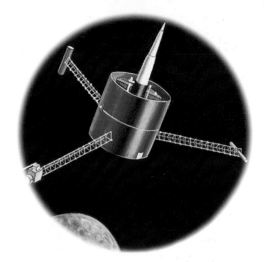

In the future, people may travel to the Moon to live and work. We may build giant spacecraft in orbit around the Moon to carry astronauts to the distant planets. We may dig valuable minerals out of the Moon's rocks. Astronomers would like to build telescopes on the far side of the Moon. From there, they would have a fantastic view of the stars.

Lunar Prospector probe

In 1998, Prospector found ice and water on the Moon. This water could be used to help launch rockets from the Moon.

Mining on the Moon

Valuable minerals could be mined on the Moon and sent back to Earth. Moon miners would live in a specially built Moon base and wear a spacesuit to go to work.

Delivering oxygen plant

Building oxygen plant

Building living quarters

Arrival of crew

Living and working on the Moon

Glossary

aerial A length of wire, a metal frame or a dish-shaped sheet of metal used to send or receive radio signals.

Apollo American space project that landed astronauts on the Moon.

basalt Volcanic rock made from hardened lava; the most common rock on the Earth and the Moon.

billion One thousand million.

breccia Rock made from soil and rock squeezed together when hit by a falling object.

corona The Sun's atmosphere, only visible during a solar eclipse.

gibbous Part of a circle – bigger than half a circle but smaller than a whole circle.

maria Latin name meaning seas; used by early astronomers for the dark patches on the Moon's surface which they thought may contain water.

module One complete part, or section, of a spacecraft.

molten Melted; molten rock is also called lava.

orbit The endless path of a spacecraft around the Moon, the Moon around the Earth, or any planet around the Sun.

oxygen A gas with no colour or smell. We need oxygen to breathe in order to live.

rille A long, thin valley on the Moon carved out by flowing lava.

Sea of Tranquillity The part of the Moon where the first astronauts landed in July 1969.

Space Age The time since 4th October 1957, when the first artificial satellite, Sputnik 1, was launched into space around the Earth.

tides The twice daily movement of the sea up onto the shore and down again caused by the pull of the Moon's gravity.

waning Seeming to grow smaller.

waxing Seeming to grow larger.

Lunar and solar eclipses	Date	Type	Can be seen from:
	28th July 1999	Lunar	North and South America, Asia, Australia
	11th August 1999	Solar	Europe, India, Middle East
	21st January 2000	Lunar	The Americas, Asia, Australia, East Africa
	5th February 2000	Solar	Antarctica
	1st July 2000	Solar	Far South Pacific Ocean, Patagonia
	16th July 2000	Lunar	Asia, Australia, Pacific Ocean
	31st July 2000	Solar	Siberia, North Pole, Alaska, northern Canada, Greenland
	25th December 2000	Solar	North America
	9th January 2001	Lunar	Africa, Europe, Asia
	21st June 2001	Solar	South Atlantic Ocean, southern Africa, Madagascar
	5th July 2001	Lunar	East Africa, Asia, Australia
	14th December 2001	Solar	Pacific Ocean, Costa Rica
	30th December 2001	Lunar	Asia, Australia, the Americas

Index